WHY WE CELEBRATE CHINESE NEW YEAR

Chinese New Year

Everything to Know about Your Favorite Holiday

EUGENIA CHU

Illustrations by **JAVIERA MAC-LEAN**

an imprint of Sourcebooks

Copyright © 2025 by Callisto Publishing LLC
Cover and internal design © 2025 by Callisto Publishing LLC
Illustrations © Javiera Mac-lean with the following exception:
© I_Mak/Shutterstock: cover (banner)
Series Designer: Elizabeth Zuhl
Art Director: Elizabeth Zuhl
Art Producer: Samantha Ulban
Editor: Alyson Penn
Production Editor: Andrew Yackira
Production Manager: Martin Worthington

Callisto Kids and the colophon are registered trademarks of Callisto Publishing LLC.

All rights reserved. No part of this book may be reproduced in any form or by any electronic or mechanical means including information storage and retrieval systems—except in the case of brief quotations embodied in critical articles or reviews—without permission in writing from its publisher, Sourcebooks LLC.

Published by Callisto Publishing LLC C/O Sourcebooks LLC
P.O. Box 4410, Naperville, Illinois 60567-4410
(630) 961-3900
callistopublishing.com

Originally published as *Celebrating Chinese New Year* in 2021 in the United States of America by Callisto Kids, an imprint of Callisto Publishing LLC. This edition issued based on the paperback edition published in 2021 by Callisto Kids, an imprint of Callisto Publishing LLC.

Library of Congress Cataloging-in-Publication Data is on file with the publisher.

This product conforms to all applicable CPSC and CPSIA standards.

Source of Production: Wing King Tong Paper Products Co. Ltd. Shenzhen, Guangdong Province, China
Date of Production: May 2024
Run Number: 5040113

Printed and bound in China.
WKT 10 9 8 7 6 5 4 3 2 1

To my Brandon—my inspiration
and the reason I write

CONTENTS

What Is Chinese
New Year?
1

History and
Folklore
2

Preparation
8

How to
Celebrate
16

Around
the World
22

Culture
Corner
27

Learn to Say It!
36

Glossary
37

Resources
40

WHAT IS CHINESE NEW YEAR?

Chinese New Year, also called the Spring Festival or Lunar New Year, is the most celebrated holiday in China. Chinese New Year is similar to other Lunar New Year celebrations that take place in Asia and around the world. The new year is a time when people open their homes to friends and family to mark the end of winter and the coming of spring.

The holiday starts on the first day of the **lunisolar calendar** when the new moon comes out, and lasts for 15 days until the next full moon rises. The lunisolar calendar is based on the movements of the moon and sun and the seasons, so Chinese New Year falls on a different day each year, usually between January 21 and February 20.

HISTORY AND FOLKLORE

No one knows when people started celebrating Chinese New Year, but the **traditions** go back more than 3,000 years! Before modern times, China had **dynasties**, or families of rulers. Some say Chinese New Year began during the Shang Dynasty (1600–1046 BCE), when people offered religious sacrifices to their ancestors and gods in order to pray for blessings each year. During the Zhou Dynasty (1046–256 BCE), the celebrations became social as well.

The Chinese New Year date was set sometime during the Han Dynasty (202 BCE–220 CE). During this time, revelers burned bamboo to create loud, crackling noises to drive away evil.

During the Wei and Jin Dynasties (220–420 CE), Chinese New Year became even more of a social event. People started the New Year's Eve customs of cleaning the house, staying up late, and having big family dinners.

Over time, more fun customs developed, like setting off firecrackers and visiting relatives and friends. Today, Chinese New Year is an official holiday in China and is celebrated all around the world!

THE LEGEND BEHIND CHINESE NEW YEAR

The most popular ancient legend tells of a horrible sea monster named Nian. (**Nián (年)** means "year" in Chinese.) At the end of each year, Nian came ashore in China to eat crops, farm animals, and even villagers. The villagers began hiding in the mountains to escape Nian. One year, an old man stayed behind and waited for Nian. He taped red paper to the doors, wore red clothes, and burned bamboo to make a loud crackling sound. At midnight, Nian came and heard all the noise and saw red everywhere! Nian was so frightened, the monster ran back to the sea, never to return. Since then, to welcome in the new year, people wear red clothes, tape red paper to the doors, light firecrackers, and happily shout, "**Gōngxǐ Gōngxǐ (恭喜 恭喜)! Xīnnián kuàilè (新年快乐)**!" which means "Congratulations! Happy New Year!"

THE ZODIAC CALENDAR

Each lunar year is named after one of the 12 **Chinese Zodiac** animals: rat, ox, tiger, rabbit, dragon, snake, horse, sheep/goat (in Chinese, the word for sheep and goat is the same), monkey, rooster, dog, and pig. People born in that year are thought to have the qualities associated with that year's animal. For example,

On Chinese New Year, everyone turns a year older—no matter when they were actually born.

if you were born in 2020 (or 2008, 1996, 1984, etc.), the Year of the Rat, it is believed you will be optimistic, energetic, clever, and successful.

Why these animals and why in this order? In one popular legend, the Jade Emperor, who was known as "the Ruler of Heaven" in Chinese folklore, decided that animals would become part of the calendar and held a race. The first 12 animals to come across the river would have one year of the zodiac named after them.

The rat and cat, who were best friends, were worried because they were not good swimmers. They hatched a plan to ride across the river on top of the ox, who was a powerful swimmer. As the ox neared the finish line, the rat leapt ahead, knocking the cat off the ox,

The highlight of Chinese New Year parades is the dragon dance, because dragons are a Chinese symbol of good luck.

and came in first. Poor cat! The ox came in second, followed by the tiger, the rabbit, the dragon, the snake, the horse, the sheep/goat, the monkey, the rooster, the dog, and finally, the pig. The cat never made it! Since then, cats have disliked rats and are terrified of water.

PREPARATION

How you enter the Chinese New Year sets the tone for the upcoming year, so it is important to start off right.

One of the best ways to create a fresh start before the holiday is to clean the house. By sweeping away the dust and throwing away things that you don't need anymore, you say goodbye to the old year. Celebrators clear away the previous year's bad luck and make space for the new year's good luck.

Many people also clean themselves and get their hair cut before the new year to look their best for all the festivities, visits, and photos. Some people also get haircuts because they believe using sharp objects during the 15-day celebration will cut out good **fortune** for the coming year.

A new year means new beginnings, so there is lots of shopping, buying new clothes and shoes to wear—especially in red, because red means good luck. People also buy gifts for family and friends, decorations for the house, lanterns, and lots of food!

Another important Chinese New Year preparation is to decorate houses, shops, and restaurants with red lanterns, red **couplets** (Chinese blessings written on red paper), paper cutouts, Chinese knots, pictures of the lucky zodiac animal of the year, and paintings. Communities put these decorations up to ward off evil, a custom that may go back to the legend of Nian the sea monster, and to welcome long life, good health, wealth, and peace. Many families make their own fun decorations, banners, and signs with New Year's greetings and good luck symbols.

Celebrators also try to repay all debts, return borrowed things, and forgive friends and enemies alike. Kids even catch up with all their homework. This way, they can start the new year without anything holding them back. Now everyone is ready to welcome a brand-new year full of happiness, health, and good fortune!

Flowers are placed around the house to symbolize rebirth and growth before and during Chinese New Year.

On New Year's Eve, family members from near and far gather for a huge dinner feast with lots of dishes to give blessings for the next year! The meal can take many days to prepare, so they start early. Food is especially important during Chinese New Year because it signifies **prosperity** and abundance for the coming year. The feast dishes are symbols for wealth, happiness, long life, and success.

After the New Year's Eve dinner, parents and grandparents give children—both younger kids and unmarried adults—red envelopes, called **hóngbāo (红包)**, which contain money. The amount of money is usually in round numbers or numbers ending in 8, a lucky number; the amount never ends in a 4, an unlucky number, because "4" in Chinese sounds like the word for "death." Before receiving their *hóngbāo* (红包), kids approach the adults and, with respect and glee, say *"Xīnnián kuàilè* (新年快乐)! **Gōngxǐ fā cái (恭喜发财)**!" or "Happy New Year! Congratulations and prosperity!" Afterward, everyone stays up late to count down to the new year.

To avoid bad luck for the year, many people avoid using knives or scissors or borrowing money during the Chinese New Year season.

Some people light firecrackers at midnight to send off the old year and start off the new with a burst of color and noise that scares off evil spirits and welcomes good luck.

YOU ARE WHAT YOU EAT

Every region in China serves different foods, but here are a few of the common feast dishes:

1. Chinese dumplings, or **jiǎozi (饺子)**, represent wealth and prosperity. They are shaped like gold ingots, which were used as money in ancient China.

2. Spring rolls, or **chūnjuǎn (春卷)**, represent prosperity or wealth because they look like gold bars.

3. Noodles, especially long noodles called longevity noodles, or **chángshòu miàn (长寿面)**, represent long life. The longer the noodle, the luckier you are!

4. Steamed fish represents surplus (having more than you need) and wealth because in Chinese, the word "fish," or **yú (鱼)**, sounds the same as **yú (余)**, which means "extra" or "surplus."

5. **Niángāo (年糕)** means "New Year cake" and represents different kinds of growth—a rise in business, a growth in career or income, or children getting taller or earning better grades.

6. Certain round and golden fruits, like tangerines and oranges, represent fullness, wealth, and family unity. Also, the Chinese word for "orange," **chéng (橙)**, sounds the same spoken out loud as the word for "success," **chéng (成)**. Another word for "orange" is júzi (橘子), which sounds like the word for "good luck," **jí (吉)**.

HOW TO CELEBRATE

China celebrates their new year for 15 days with parties, parades, and other events. On the last day, the Lantern Festival is held and often highlighted by a dragon dance.

Children relax, play with their friends, wear their new red clothes, receive gifts, play games, go to fun events, and plan how to spend their *hóngbāo* (红包) money. Another popular tradition is making Chinese dumplings, or *jiǎozi* (饺子). Many families also travel to visit relatives who live far away.

Some families love to go to fairs that sell street food and watch parades with dragon and lion dances. Many people confuse these two dances, but dragon and lion dances are very different! Dragon dancers hold the dragon up on poles and chase a pearl held by another dancer, whereas the lion dance usually has two dancers inside a lion costume. Children feed the lions vegetables and *hóngbāo* (红包), and often, the lions will let kids pet them! The loud drumming and clashing cymbals for both dances are super cool, and many believe they chase away bad luck and evil spirits.

Each day of Chinese New Year has its own traditions. Even though the United States does not give people 15 days off from work or school for this holiday, you can still celebrate with many of the following customs at home, at work, and at school:

> At midnight, all the doors and windows are opened to let the old year out.

DAY 1

On Chinese New Year's Day, people rest, relax, and eat feast leftovers—yum! To avoid washing away good luck for the year, cooking, cleaning the house, and washing hair are **taboo**, or forbidden, on this day.

DAYS 2 TO 13

You can honor traditions during these days in many different ways. Celebrations vary across different families. For example, adults can make offerings to the God of Wealth and the **Kitchen God** on day 4, break taboos by sweeping everything away on day 5, and visit family and friends during these two weeks. And, of course, older relatives can give children and unmarried adults *hóngbāo* (红包).

DAY 14

On day 14, celebrators prepare lanterns for the next day's **Lantern Festival**.

Over a billion people travel for Chinese New Year, the world's largest annual human migration!

DAY 15

This is the last day of the Chinese New Year celebration, which ends with the Lantern Festival. Families and friends stroll under the first full moon of the year holding lanterns, or they go to festivals filled with beautiful and bright lanterns in all shapes, sizes, and colors. Afterward, they enjoy **tangyuan (汤圆)**, sweet rice balls that look like round little moons brewed in a soup.

THE 15 DAYS OF CHINESE NEW YEAR

DAY 1
Relax

DAY 2
Visit family and friends

DAY 3
Stay home and avoid disagreements and arguments

DAY 4
Make offerings to the God of Wealth and the Kitchen God

DAY 5
Break the New Year's taboos by sweeping and cleaning

DAY 6
Drive away the Ghost of Poverty by discarding old clothes

DAY 7
Eat healthy foods symbolizing long life, prosperity, and abundance

DAY 8
Celebrate rice, China's staple food

DAY 9
Celebrate the birthday of the Jade Emperor, the Ruler of Heaven

DAYS 10 TO 12
Continue visiting family and friends

DAY 13
Eat vegetarian dishes to help cleanse and soothe the tummy

DAY 14
Prepare and make lanterns for the next day's Lantern Festival

DAY 15
Lantern Festival

AROUND THE WORLD

ou may have heard Chinese New Year also called "Lunar New Year." Lunar New Year celebrates the start of the lunar or lunisolar year.

It can be celebrated by anyone who follows the moon cycle calendar. For example, Korea, Vietnam, and Singapore all have their own Lunar New Year celebrations with traditions that are different from Chinese New Year. People around the world celebrate both Chinese New Year and Lunar New Year!

In China, nearly every city, town, and village celebrates Chinese New Year—and some have special traditions. In Ditan Park in Beijing, people watch

reenactments of religious ceremonies, in which ancient rulers offer ritual sacrifices to the God of the Earth.

Here in the United States, many larger cities, especially those with a Chinatown like San Francisco and Chicago, have parades with lion dances and yummy food! Boston has a Chinese New Year Flower Market. In New York City, revelers light 600,000 firecrackers to ward off evil spirits. That's a lot of noise!

In Sydney, Australia, the Chinese New Year Festival includes pop-up markets, dances, food festivals, street parties, dragon boat racing, and film festivals. Sydney also lights up its most famous landmarks, like the Sydney Harbour Bridge and the Opera House, in red.

More fireworks are used during Chinese New Year than any other time or event in the world—even more than the Fourth of July!

In Paris, France, the Eiffel Tower glows red for Chinese New Year, and the city's most famous street, the Champs-Élysées, is lined with floats, firecrackers, dancing dragons, and other performers.

Besides Christmas, Chinese New Year is the most celebrated holiday in the world. See if you can find a celebration near you and join in the fun. Or have your own Chinese New Year celebration with your friends!

CULTURE CORNER

Chinese New Year is a special occasion when people get to participate in many exciting crafts, activities, and recipes. Try these at home with family or friends to join the celebration.

CHINESE DUMPLINGS

Chinese dumplings, or *jiǎozi* (饺子), are made and eaten throughout the year, but especially during Chinese New Year. The two most common ways to cook dumplings are to panfry or boil them. Instructions for both methods are below. Ask a parent or other adult to help before you start cooking.

Makes: 40 to 50 | **Prep Time:** 30 to 45 minutes
Cook time: 15 to 20 minutes

⅔ pound ground pork

2 cups chopped spinach

⅓ cup chopped Chinese chives or scallions

1½ tablespoons soy sauce

1½ tablespoons sesame oil

½ tablespoon oil, plus more as needed for panfrying

½ teaspoon salt

¼ teaspoon black pepper

Premade dumpling wrappers (found at Asian grocery stores and some supermarkets)

1. In a large mixing bowl, combine the pork, spinach, chives, soy sauce, both oils, salt, and pepper. Mix well.
2. Put about 1 teaspoon of filling in each wrapper. Flatten the filling a bit in the center.
3. Wet the edges of the wrapper with a little water.
4. Fold and pinch the edges of the wrapper together to keep the filling inside.

TO PANFRY:

1. Heat 1 to 2 tablespoons of cooking oil in a pan on medium-high heat. When the oil is hot, place the dumplings into the pan, leaving about 1/8 inch between them because they will plump up.
2. Fry until the bottoms are golden brown.
3. Add 1/3 cup of water, or more if needed to have about 1/4 inch of water in the pan, and cover with a lid. Steam for 5 to 7 minutes, until the dumplings begin to sizzle.
4. Remove the lid. The dumplings should look translucent, or see-through. Fry a bit longer, until the bottoms are crispy.

TO BOIL:

1. Bring a large pot of water to a boil. Place the dumplings gently into the boiling water.
2. Once the water returns to a boil and the dumplings are floating, add 1/2 cup of cold water and leave uncovered.
3. Let the water come to a boil again, and add another 1/2 cup of cold water.
4. When the water returns to a boil for the third time, the dumplings are done! Remove them immediately so the wrappers don't get mushy.

PAPER CHINESE LANTERNS

Making paper lanterns is fun and easy! Finish one and hang it somewhere special, or make a bunch and string them all together to decorate a larger area.

Construction paper

Scissors

Glue, tape, or stapler

Optional: String (if you want to make several lanterns and string them together)

1. Take a sheet of construction paper and cut a strip from the long edge. This strip will be used for the handle.
2. Fold the paper in half lengthwise.
3. Cut through the fold, but not all the way. (Do not cut the strip off.) Make several cuts from one end to the other.
4. Unfold the paper.
5. Roll the paper so it forms a cylinder, and tape, glue, or staple the ends together.
6. Tape, glue, or staple the handle on. Now you're done!
7. **Optional:** If you want to make several lanterns to string together, tape them onto a long piece of string, and then hang. Beautiful!

CHINESE DRUMS

The drum, or **gǔ (鼓)**, is used in lots of Chinese music. This particular drum, called a pellet drum, has two drum faces with two pellets connected to each side. It is played by turning the stick attached to the drum so that the two pellets swing back and forth, hitting the two drum faces.

2 paper plates
Paint, markers, or crayons
Stickers (optional)
Tape or glue

Sturdy stick, chopstick, or wooden rod
2 bells or beads
String
Stapler or glue

1. Decorate the backs of the plates with paint, markers, crayons, and stickers, if you wish.
2. Tape the stick to the inside of one plate.
3. Make the pellets by tying a bell or bead to one end of two pieces of string.
4. Tape the other end of the string to the inside edge of the plates.
5. Staple or glue the two plates together.
6. Play by turning the drum. Rub the stick between your hands to drum faster! Try dancing to the beat of the drum.

PAPER BAG CHINESE DRAGONS

In China, the dragon is a symbol of good luck, long life, and wisdom. There are always dragon dances at Chinese New Year festivals. Now you can make your own.

Decorations like fabric shapes, feathers, leaves, ribbons, felt, and tissue paper

Glue

Paper lunch bag

Red and yellow construction paper

Paint, markers, or crayons

Scissors

1. Select items to glue to the edges of the bottom of the paper bag, which will be the edges of the dragon's face. Use the items listed, cut out shapes, or trace your hands on construction paper and cut them out—whatever you like!

2. Glue the items to the paper bag's bottom, making sure they extend beyond the edges of the bottom of the bag.

3. Using the construction paper, cut an oval shape the size of the paper bag's bottom.

4. Draw a face for the dragon on the oval shape.

5. Glue the oval onto the bottom of the paper bag, covering the other items except for where they extend beyond the bag.

6. Decorate the rest of the paper bag, for the dragon's body.

7. Now you are ready to play and dance with your dragon!

CHOPSTICK PICKUP GAME

This is a fun game to play with your family and friends. The only catch: You have to use chopsticks!

EACH PLAYER WILL NEED:

A pair of chopsticks

Two bowls

Small pom-poms, mini marshmallows, wrapped candies, or other small items

1. Give each player a pair of chopsticks and two bowls. (Plastic is best.)
2. Fill one bowl for each player with the same items.
3. Using only chopsticks, each player must move the items from one bowl to the other.
4. Whoever transfers all the items first wins!

Fun tip: To make this game more challenging, place the bowls several feet apart and have each player carry the items from one bowl to the other.

CHINESE ZODIAC CALENDAR

Do you remember the story about how the 12 zodiac animals were chosen and how each year is represented by one of them? Well, now you can keep track by making your own Chinese zodiac calendar!

Paper plate or construction paper, cut into a circle (a light color, like white or yellow, is best)

Ruler

Markers or crayons

Small pictures of the 12 zodiac animals (optional)

Tape

1. Take the paper plate or construction paper circle. Fold it in half, then in half again. Then fold it into thirds. When you unfold it, there should be 12 triangular sections.
2. Use the ruler to draw lines where the folds are, to mark off the 12 sections.
3. Draw the zodiac animals at the top of each section in this order: rat, pig, dog, rooster, monkey, sheep/goat, horse, snake, dragon, rabbit, tiger, and ox. Instead of drawing, you can also cut out pictures of the animals and tape them into the 12 sections.
4. Write the name of each animal next to the corresponding picture.
5. **Optional:** In addition to writing each animal in English, try writing it in Chinese, too!
6. In the center, list the years corresponding to each zodiac animal. List as many or as few years as you like. Remember, each animal is represented every 12 years.

CHINESE ZODIAC NAMES

RAT
鼠

MONKEY
猴

DRAGON
龙

PIG
猪

SHEEP/GOAT
羊

RABBIT
兔

DOG
狗

HORSE
马

TIGER
虎

ROOSTER
鸡

SNAKE
蛇

OX
牛

LEARN TO SAY IT!

Here are a few common phrases people say to each other during Chinese New Year:

Xīnnián kuàilè
新年快乐
HAPPY NEW YEAR

Gōngxǐ fā cái
恭喜发财
CONGRATULATIONS AND WISHING YOU PROSPERITY

Hóngbāo ná lái
红包拿来
BRING THE RED ENVELOPE

Shēn tǐ jiàn kāng
身体健康
WISHING YOU GOOD HEALTH

Hé jiā xìng fú
阖家幸福
WISHING YOU A HAPPY FAMILY

GLOSSARY

chángshòu miàn (长寿面): longevity noodles

chéng (橙): orange

chéng (成): success

Chinese Zodiac: a 12-year cycle based on the lunar calendar that assigns an animal and its qualities to each year

chūnjuǎn (春卷): spring rolls

couplet: two complementary poetic lines, often written on red paper and posted on doors during Chinese New Year

dynasty: a family of rulers in a country

fortune: wealth, happiness, longevity, or good luck

gǔ (鼓): drum

hóngbāo (红包): red envelopes containing money, given to children and unmarried adults for good luck and good wishes during Chinese New Year

jí (吉): good luck

jiǎozi (饺子): Chinese dumplings

Kitchen God: an important Chinese god who protects the home and family and to whom families offer sacrifices before Chinese New Year, so they will get high marks when the Kitchen God reports back to the Jade Emperor (the Ruler of Heaven) on New Year's Day

Lantern Festival: a Chinese festival honoring ancestors, promoting peace and forgiveness, and marking the return of spring that is celebrated on the fifteenth and last day of Chinese New Year, during the first full moon

lunisolar calendar: a calendar based on the phases of the moon (moon's orbit around Earth), the movement of the sun (Earth's orbit around the sun), and the seasons

nián (年): year; also, the name of the sea monster from Chinese legend

niángāo (年糕): New Year cake

prosperity: the state of being successful, thriving, or wealthy, or having a rich and full life and good fortune

taboo: a custom that is forbidden

tangyuan (汤圆): sweet rice balls shaped like round little moons and brewed in a soup

tradition: a custom, behavior, or practice that has a special significance, is passed down through the generations, or is done regularly year after year

yú (鱼): fish

yú (余): extra or surplus

RESOURCES

Miss Panda Chinese: MissPandaChinese.com

Scholastic Chinese New Year Activities: Scholastic.com/teachers/articles/teaching-content/chinese-new-year-activity-ideas

Educational Resources: Education.com/resources/chinese-new-year

Chinese New Year website: ChineseNewYear.net

Museum of Chinese in America: MOCANYC.org

Chalk Academy: ChalkAcademy.com

ABOUT THE AUTHOR

After years of working as an attorney, **Eugenia Chu** became a stay-at-home mom and then a writer. She is a first-generation Chinese American citizen and lives in Miami Beach with her husband and her son, Brandon. Brandon is the inspiration for her books, which all include some Chinese culture and language. Chu is also the author of *Brandon Makes Jiǎo Zi* (餃子), a picture book, and two chapter books, *Brandon Goes to Beijing* (北京) and *Brandon Goes to Hong Kong* (香港).

Learn more at EugeniaChu.com.

ABOUT THE ILLUSTRATOR

Illustrator **Javiera Mac-lean** has written and illustrated two of her own children's books, *The Cloud in the Window* and *Folding Adventure*, both published by Bibliográfica Internacional, as well as other books related to child psychology. She has also illustrated for multinational companies and magazines in the United States, Chile, and Spain. In 2017 she studied illustration at the EINA School. You can see her work on Instagram @JavieraMaclean.